Read and Write

Like a Professor

A companion to
The Professor's Book of Readings

I0164809

By Sara Tusek

International Leadership Institute Publications

Florida and Prague

Copyright 2020 by International Leadership Institute Publications

Sara D. Tusek, Executive Editor

International Leadership Institute Publications

PO Box 950-788, Lake Mary, FL 32795-0788

USA

www.ili.cc

Publication History:

First print edition, 2020

ISBN: 978-0-9786337-8-3

First e-book edition, 2021

Cover and text design: Noah Shepherd, NY, NY

Published by International Leadership Institute Publications:

The Professor's Book of Readings. Sara Tusek. International Leadership Institute Publications, Lake Mary, FL, 2021.

Read and Write Like a Professor. Sara Tusek. International Leadership Institute Publications, Lake Mary, FL, 2020.

Reinventing Your Future. Jaroslav B. Tusek and Sara Tusek. International Leadership Institute Publications, Lake Mary, FL, 2019.

Leaders to Follow. Jaroslav B. Tusek with Sara Tusek. International Leadership Institute Publications, Lake Mary, FL, 2018.

Prague for Beginners: Finding Myself in Prague. Sara Tusek. International Leadership Institute Publications, Lake Mary, FL, 2017.

21st Century Jobs. Jaroslav B. Tusek and Sara Tusek. International Leadership Institute Publications, Lake Mary, FL, 2009.

From Idea to Book in Five Steps. Sara Tusek. International Leadership Institute Publications, Lake Mary, FL, 2019.

Three Things You Can't Do in Prague. Jaroslav B. Tusek and Sara Tusek. Servant Leaders Press, Ponte Vedra Beach, FL, 2006.

Your Career Passport. Jaroslav B. Tusek and Sara D. Shepherd (Tusek). International Leadership Institute Publications, Ponte Vedra Beach, FL, 2nd Edition, 1993; 1st Edition, 1991.

Leaders to Follow, 1991-2012; *Business Briefs,* 1992-1997; *Careers,* 1987-2012; *Servant Leaders,* 2005-2012; *continuous conversion,* 2006-2012; *ALOE: A Lesson on English,* 2007-2012.

Other publications:

East Tennessee Business Journal/Chattanooga Business Journal, contributing editors and columnists, 1993-2008.

College to First Job: Step by Step. Sara D. Shepherd (Tusek). The University of the South, Sewanee, TN, 1988.

Looking Ahead. Sara D. Shepherd (Tusek). The University of the South, Sewanee, TN, 1988.

Career Development Handbook. Sara D. Shepherd (Tusek). The University of the South, Sewanee, TN, 1987.

Designing Your Future. Jaroslav B. Tusek. St. Lawrence University, Canton, NY, 1985.

Career Development Kit for Future Leaders: An Introduction to Career Management. Jaroslav B. Tusek. American Management Association, Hamilton, NY, 1984.

Career Search Kit for International Students: A Handbook of Sources for the International Job Market. Jaroslav B. Tusek. New York Institute of Technology, New York, NY, 1983.

Job Search Kit for the 80s. Jaroslav B. Tusek. New York Institute of Technology, New York, NY, 1981.

Table of Contents

Welcome from Professor Tusek!

Thank you for buying this practical handbook on academic reading and writing, *Read and Write Like a Professor*. I've made this book short, simple, and easy to use so that you can start improving your reading and writing skills right away.

You can benefit most by using this book as a companion to the anthology I edited, *The Professor's Book of Readings*. In *The Professor's Book of Readings*, you have access to a variety of texts: short essays, stories, poems, and analytical articles.

Each short reading in *The Professor's Book of Readings* has three writing prompts that coordinate with activities in this book, *Read and Write Like a Professor*. Through practice in reading and writing, your skills will grow, and your confidence will blossom.

I've been teaching English Composition and Literature on the university, college, and secondary levels for more than 35 years. In that time, I've worked with thousands of students from dozens of countries in North America, Europe, the Caribbean, Africa, Asia, and Central and South America.

My students bring with them a wide variety of experience, skills, and confidence in reading and writing in English, and I have created techniques and strategies for teaching each student as an individual.

Working with so many different people has given me practical knowledge of the most important skills in becoming a competent reader and writer using the English language. This handbook is built to help you develop and practice these skills.

The companion book, *The Professor's Book of Readings*, provides texts that you can read and respond to, helping you build essential communication strategies. The readings give you something specific to write about, so you can develop the skills to write with focus, clarity, and unity of purpose.

Please visit my website at www.ili.cc to get an overview of what my business, the International Leadership Institute, offers to all leaders, current or aspiring, in terms of building communication and cross-cultural skills that will lead to success in whatever they choose to do in life. . You can also see other books we've published that may be of interest to you.

I would appreciate your feedback on how this book has helped you improve your skills and gain knowledge of the importance of reading and writing well in academic settings. You can email me at the address on the Contact page of the website.

Good luck in your endeavors to become a more effective reader and writer!

Note: I use third person pronouns (they, their, them) when I write about an individual rather than he, she, or any pronoun that presupposes gender. Some writing teachers will not find this acceptable. I leave it to you to decide for yourself what makes sense.

Chapter One: Reading to gain information, develop critical thinking skills, and experience effective writing strategies

Chapter Highlights

- Reading develops your writing skills

- Close reading and annotation

- Reading for pleasure

Reading develops your writing skills

Reading well is the key to writing well. Writers produce written texts which are then read; your own experiences as a reader sharpen your ideas of what good writing looks like and point you toward the strategies needed to be an effective, interesting writer.

Reading serves many purposes, but all reading is primarily a form of communication. When you read, you enter a conversation with the author. If what you're reading interests you, you'll find yourself cheering when the writer says something funny, insightful, or wise. You'll wish you could ask the writer to explain a point or tell you more about a good example.

Why is it so important to read if you want to be a better writer? Here are valuable skills you develop by reading. Following this list is a discussion of each skill.

- *See what interesting, effective writing looks like by consciously and subconsciously absorbing the elements of good writing.*

- *Learn how other writers arrange their writing so that the reader can follow the main points and arguments of the text.*

- *Gain new information if your writing assignments calls for research: facts, dates, statistics, laws, significant events, and key players.*

- *Enlarge your vocabulary through using context clues.*

- *Develop critical thinking skills by evaluating what you read as to its credibility, usefulness, relevance, and organization.*

Each of these skills is needed for good writing on the academic level. The good news is that the skills work together and reinforce each other, so that as you build one skill set, all your skills improve.

See what interesting, effective writing looks like by consciously and subconsciously absorbing the elements of good writing

When you read, you make constant judgments as to whether or not the writer is engaging your attention. These judgments often are subconscious—that is, you want to read on when the writing is easy to follow and has enough

3

action to be interesting. If the writing is poorly presented or dull, or if the information is too dense and not well-organized, you may lose interest quickly and have to grit your teeth to get through it.

As you read, stop yourself periodically to evaluate what you just read. Did that last sentence make sense, or did you have to read it a few times to understand it? Are the writer's ideas clear, or do you have to struggle to find them? Are the sentences well-constructed? Does each paragraph make its point with conviction? Has the writer given enough detail (examples, facts, or description) that you can envision what they write about?

If you give close consideration to what you read, you will grow as a writer. Rather than just seeing a text as words, you will begin to notice patterns of organization that work well. You will pick out poorly-formed, clumsy sentences and notice when paragraphs go on and on without making a point.

With very little conscious effort on your part, each text you read serves as a model for you as a writer. Whatever irritates you is a clue as to what you must be careful about when you write; whatever delights you shows how to make your reader smile!

Learn how other writers arrange their writing so that the reader can follow the main points and arguments of the text

Here the emphasis is on noticing how writers control what they write. Just writing down ideas one after another produces a "laundry list" of information. Good ideas are essential to good writing, but it's just as important that ideas be linked together and follow some pattern of development.

You can group ideas many ways: by topic, by when or where they originated, by how much impact they have had on other ideas, and so on. For example, you can take a simple idea and develop it by defining it, giving an example of it, finding its flaws, or showing how it's been used. Knowing how to organize and develop ideas is a key skill; ask yourself how skilled in this regard is the writer whose work you are reading.

Obviously, good organization is crucial in textbooks and essays, but it's also necessary in creative writing such as novels, poems, and short stories. Even blank verse poetry, which seems to have no rules, has a structure that guides the reader to the writer's main ideas.

Gain new information if your writing assignments calls for research: facts, dates, statistics, laws, significant events, and key players. Enlarge your vocabulary through using context clues

Often, what you read (especially for an academic class) is intended to provide you with new information. Reading to gain information needs to be done deliberately and systematically. Your main goal is to identify key information and incorporate it into your own way of thinking about and understanding of the topic or the information.

As you read complex or dense texts such as academic readings or textbooks, be sure to use context clues to decipher the meaning of unfamiliar words and technical terms. You can use a dictionary, but just being able to recite a dictionary definition does not mean that you understand the word. Using context clues (noticing the words around a new word) helps you comprehend a word's use and function.

At the same time, you can annotate the text so that you remember and absorb key information and ideas. You will find tips on annotating in *Appendix A: Basic tools for reading and writing: creating a thesis; annotating, outlining, summarizing, and analyzing.*

Here are three proven strategies for effective reading when the goal is to increase your knowledge. As you read, keep in mind that you are doing all three things simultaneously:

- Locating the most *important information*;

- Making sure you *understand that information* by writing a brief summary or explaining it to someone else;

- Finding ways to immediately *use the information*: quiz yourself, write a poem about it, draw a diagram of it, and so on.

Develop critical thinking skills by evaluating what you read as to its credibility, usefulness, relevance, and organization

When you think critically, you question what you are reading. Rather than think it must be true if it's in print, you read with an eye to deciding whether or not to believe or agree with what you read. Here are some tips on reading critically:

- Imagine that you are having a conversation with the writer. What would you ask them?

- Where did the writer get this information? Is the writer an expert whose words carry authority or simply someone offering an opinion? Is the writer a credible source of information?

- Hidden in most writing are the author's biases and presuppositions. Pick out bias (instances in which the writer's attitude toward the subject is influenced by their own thinking and opinions) and presuppositions (what does the writer seem to think you already know or believe?).

- How up-to-date is the information? Is it still relevant, or has the situation changed so much that the information is useless for your purposes?

- Look for the writer's thesis (main point). It may be stated clearly, or it may be implied (you have to figure it out from hints and patterns in the writing). Does the entire text work together to prove the thesis?

- Identify, as a reader, what is effective and what is ineffective in what you read. Are the paragraphs so long they are discouraging? Is the writing well-ordered? Does the writer make sure you understand one thing before going on to another?

- Consider the text as a unified whole. What is the writer's purpose? How does the writer use paragraph development, vocabulary, and rhetorical devices to achieve that purpose?

- Become a "friendly critic" of the writer and the text. Evaluate the text for the organization of the writing, the writer's ability to communicate to the reader and keep the reader engaged, and the value of the information provided.

Close Reading and Annotation

When you read, ask yourself why you are reading. If it's simply for entertainment, then read away! But if you need to learn something new, be able to use new information, or write about the reading, you need to slow down and read closely. Here are valuable strategies for close reading:

- *Preview the text:* Look at the name of the writer and any background information provided. Locate the publishing data: name of publisher, date, location, and so on. This data gives you insight into the relevance, timeliness, and scope of the text.

- *Skim to find key points:* Quickly look over the introduction and conclusion. Read the chapter titles and headings.

- *Consider why you are reading:* Are you studying for an exam? Are you researching background information before writing a paper? Are you simply learning about something you are interested in?

- *Annotate:* Look for numbers, facts, and interesting statements. Develop a system that suits you; for guidance, look at my suggestions in *Appendix A: Basic tools for reading and writing: creating a thesis; annotating, outlining, summarizing, and analyzing.*

- *Who seems to be the intended audience?* Consider the tone (the writer's attitude: confident, authoritarian, or sarcastic, for example) and the diction (formal or informal) to understand who the writer is writing for and what that audience may already know or believe.

- *Question the writer:* How did they choose what to include? What did they not include? Does their data (facts, figures, charts) support their thesis? Do you agree with their conclusions?

- *What does the writer want you to believe?* Writing is almost always used to persuade the reader that certain things are true and others, not. The writer becomes your trusted guide; make sure the writer is trustworthy!

Reading for Pleasure

When you read for pleasure—to make the time pass when you are waiting, to relax your mind from daily routines and stresses, or to momentarily escape from your surroundings—you are building your writing skills. As a reader, you absorb important ideas and facts:

- How the writer captures and keeps your interest;
- Incidental information, as in historical fiction or mysteries set in exotic places;
- Vocabulary development and spelling;
- Sentence and paragraph development;
- How the reading is organized so that you can follow the author's thinking;

- How to read critically: is this reading good or bad? Why?

Reading for pleasure is a very effective way to absorb how writers construct their texts to be smooth, comprehensible, and pleasant to read. Consider the basics of composition (vocabulary, sentence structure, paragraph development, and punctuation) as to whether or not the writer has used them in such a way as to make the text easier to read.

You can also move on to literary analysis. Look at the text as if it were a piece of art. How has the writer "packaged" the narrative/story? It's not enough to have a good story; it must be presented in the best way possible for the reader to have maximum satisfaction.

Here are some tools of literary analysis to think about. These tools are also known as literary elements or rhetorical strategies.

- *Tone* (the writer's attitude toward the text—cynical, trusting, angry, neutral, or excited, for example);

- *Mood* (your emotional reaction to the text);

- *Setting* (time and place of the events);

- *Characters* (human and otherwise—a tree can be a character in a poem, for example);

- *Theme* (what points, topics, images, or symbols does the writer seem to keep coming back to?);

- *Plot* (the events in the narrative, usually in some kind of order as to time);

- *Figurative language*, also known as tropes (for example, metaphors, symbolism, similes, and hyperbole, which is exaggeration);

- *Additional literary devices* (including repetition, ascending or descending order of importance, point of view, or foreshadowing, etc.).

Ideally, even an academic paper should have some of the qualities and characteristics that you find in the books you read for pleasure. Your reader will appreciate any efforts you make to sustain their interest and make them wonder what's coming next, just as you appreciate your favorite writer's care in leading you through a fascinating narrative.

Reading is a complex and intriguing activity, whether for academic purposes or pleasure. Many parts of the brain are involved, and all parts of your overall humanity (emotions, spirit, and body) are touched and changed by what you read. Careful reading helps you correct your misunderstandings and lack of comprehension as you read.

As well, careful reading helps you bridge the gap between you and the writer. The text you read may be poorly-written, clumsy, or inaccurate; you can learn what not to do from this kind of reading. You will subconsciously sort what you read into examples of what works well and what is confusing or needlessly difficult for the reader of the text.

As you build your experience in reading all kinds of texts, you will improve with little conscious effort both as a reader and as a writer. This is how reading and writing work together, as every professor knows.

Activities for Reading

1. Find an article or essay that interests you in *The Professor's Book of Readings*. Using the forms in *Appendix A: Basic tools for reading and writing: annotating, outlining, summarizing, and analyzing*, do the following:

    -   Read and annotate the article.

    -   Write an outline.

    -   Write a summary. It should be about 1/3 as long as the article.

    -   Write an analysis. How are the summary and analysis alike? How are they different?

2. What is the author's main point, or thesis (also called a claim)? How can you recognize it?

3. Choose a short story or poem that you like and can understand well in *The Professor's Book of Readings*. Write a brief analysis of the text, using three of the literary analysis tools listed in this chapter. For example, you could choose setting, theme, and characters. Show

how the author uses these literary elements in the text
to build emotional resonance, create strong images, or
drive home the theme.

Chapter Two: Writing in various genres with precision and focus: academic and creative writing

Chapter Highlights

- Writing for academic purposes: essays and research papers

- Creative writing, academic and commercial

Often, we discover what we want to say in the act of saying it. This phenomenon is also true in writing. Before you write, your mind may be a muddle of thoughts, ideas, images, snapshots of memories, fragments of sentences, smells, sounds, and opinions. It may seem impossible to find clarity in such an unsorted pile of elements.

Yet the very act of writing can be the best way to sort it all out. It's often the case that formulating a thought into a coherent sequence of words leads your mind into trimming away the messy bits, leaving a clean and meaningful sentence. Then, sentence-by-sentence, you can build an essay, short story, or poem that is effectively organized, easily understandable, and full of meaning and purpose.

Writing for academic purposes: essays and research papers

In academia, each writing assignment has specific goals and purposes which may have little in common with commercial writing (popular books, plays, media articles, instruction manuals, and so on). Usually, academic writing is meant to support an argumentative thesis or to present researched data. If you fully understand the purpose of what you are being asked to write and have the needed compositional skills (sentence and paragraph formation, spelling, punctuation, and organization), you will be able to write any kind of paper called for in academic life.

Here are a few basic requirements that you, as a competent writer, must fulfill for every academic paper you write:

- Be sure that you have an original, important point (thesis) and have made your point clear to the reader;

- Master the art of combining your original thoughts and theories with the work of recognized authorities when you present research. This involves being able to correctly paraphrase key ideas and to use direct quotes to give your paper authority;

- Provide credible support for your thesis and cite any resources you use accurately and thoroughly;

- Give proper credit each time you use someone else's ideas.

Failing to give proper credit is plagiarism, a form of intellectual theft. In many academic institutions, plagiarism has a strong impact on your grade; you may have to leave a class or even the institution if you are caught plagiarizing.

Approaching a writing assignment

As you ponder over an academic assignment, think of the instructions as a short building manual for your paper. Each requirement of the assignment must be met if the paper is to stand on its own merit.

- Be sure you read all the instructions carefully. Often, there are details at the end which will influence how you approach the assignment.

- If you don't understand a detail, ask your professor or a trusted classmate to explain it. You can also consult with a tutor, either privately or in your university's Writing Center.

- If you don't understand the general purpose of the assignment, consider what you have already done in that class. Most professors construct their classes so that all assignments in some way align with each other.

- Often, a professor "scaffolds" an assignment. This means breaking it down into several steps. Each step builds on the previous step. Examine the assignment to see if it's scaffolding on what you've already done.

- If you are writing a paper, what kind of paper is it? An essay, a researched essay, a report, a discussion post, a reaction to some question or event, a case study, or a criticism of a work of art? Each of these calls for quite different organizational design. You can find definitions and guidelines for common types of essays in *Appendix B: The Essay and its genres.*

- If you have a choice of topics, think about what you would enjoy writing about. If you have no choice, think about how you could approach the assigned topic from a few different angles so as to make it more interesting for you.

Steps in composition

Regardless of what class you are taking, there are basic steps in academic writing that will lead to success. Skipping steps may seem like a way to save time, but usually you will have to go back and do them eventually, so why not do them in the right order?

If your professor has provided a text to read, use all the strategies in *Chapter One: Reading to gain information, develop critical thinking skills, and experience effective writing strategies.*

Make sure you have read and annotated the entire reading before you start writing about it—often, students in a hurry will cherry-pick the reading to find some parts that support their thesis. You are short-changing yourself and not getting full value from the reading if you don't take the time to read the entire text.

Once you have read and annotated all the texts that you will use and are sure you understand your assignment, you can begin to write!

- *Consider* your audience. You may believe that your professor is your audience, as no one else will read your paper. But imagine that you are writing to a relative or friend. How would you put the paper together so someone who's not an expert will follow your argument? This will help you expand your ability to communicate your key ideas and insights.

- It's a mistake not to *provide* sufficient context in the introductory paragraph, thinking that your professor already knows about the topic or text you are referencing. Part of your task as a writer is to convince the reader that you know what you are talking about, so be sure to set up your essay with enough background that the reader can see that you have sufficient knowledge and understanding to be trustworthy. If you are responding to a text, include the name of the text and the author's name in the introductory paragraph.

- When you *choose* your audience, you have a basis to make key decisions such as context, background, and explanation of key information. In addition, your choice of diction, tone, and mood are affected by the audience. If you are not sure how to choose your audience in an academic paper, ask your professor for advice.

- For most academic essays, *write* using formal tone. Avoid slang, abbreviations and jargon. Writing in third person (he/she/it/they) is nearly always acceptable, though some professors may allow first person (I/me/we/us) for some essays. Avoid second person (you/your). Do not use contractions: write out "do not" rather than "don't." Write out numbers up to twenty: "one," not "1."

- *Prewrite*: jot down ideas or make a "mental map" diagram (put the topic in the center and arrange ideas around it like spokes on a wheel). Free writing, bubbles, short outlines, and groupings of ideas and observations in columns are more ways to prewrite.

- *Develop* a thesis. The thesis is the main point you are trying to prove. It consists of two parts: a topic and a claim about the topic. For a full discussion of creating a thesis, read *Appendix A: Basic tools for reading and writing: creating a thesis; annotating, outlining, summarizing, and analyzing.*

- *Construct* a formal outline of your paper: introduction with thesis, body paragraphs, and conclusion. Find models in *Appendix A: Basic tools for reading and writing: creating a thesis; annotating, outlining, summarizing, and analyzing.*

- If you are using resources other than your own general knowledge (as in a research paper), *decide* where to put the quotations and paraphrased information you want to use. Remember to note where each quote and paraphrase comes from during the prewriting activities, as you must include this information in the paper.

- *Write* the first draft. This may be quite a rough draft as the goal is to get everything into the draft even if the organization is not perfect. You may find that you want to adjust your thesis as you write, sharpening it to better express your main point.

- *Self-edit* the rough draft. Use the review tools in your software program (spell-check and grammar-check). Read the draft out loud to catch omitted words, lack of clear transitions, and awkward sentences.

- *Revise* according to your self-edit.

- *Get feedback* from as many people as possible to be sure your essay is on target.

- *Complete* your final copy. Look it over again for formatting errors and typos; be sure you meet the requirements for the paper.

Qualities of an outstanding academic paper

Academic writing is meant to be factual, correct, and informative. Although most people find academic writing to be dry and dull, you will find as you read and write more extensively that you can make your writing more appealing to the reader by the use of examples and little stories that support your thesis and add liveliness to the paper. Here's a round-up of the main characteristics that need to be considered in good academic writing:

- *Purpose of the essay:* do you and the reader both understand what you are writing about and why it is important?

- *Appeal to the audience:* will your reader be able to follow your logic easily? Is your essay interesting and worth your reader's time?

- *Unity in the essay:* all parts work together to create a seamless whole;

- *Succinct introduction:* the introductory paragraph either captures the attention of the reader or leaves them confused;

- *Strong thesis:* the reader can find your thesis (often at the end of the first paragraph) and can understand its importance;

- *Logical development:* paragraphs are well-structured, and the overall essay is easy to follow;

- *Convincing conclusion:* to end the essay with a bang, repeat the thesis in different words and use the most powerful details you can find.

Creative Writing, academic and commercial

When I talk about commercial (non-academic) creative writing, I notice that I get excited and a bit apprehensive: excited because of the freedom and originality that are unleashed in writing that's not academic yet apprehensive because the familiar signposts of academic writing are gone.

Short stories, screenplays, poems, novels, comic books, flash fiction, blog entries, plays, journals, memoirs, graphic novels— all of these are forms of creative writing. In most commercially-published creative writing, there are no rules. Nearly anything goes as long as people will buy it and read it.

For you to read and write like a professor is not so crucial when you are writing for your own pleasure, for commercial purposes (to sell or publish what you write to make money) or personal development. In those cases, it's fine to let your inner creative genius take over!

However, in academia (universities and colleges, scholarly graduate fellowships and programs, ecclesiastical institutions, and the like) the accepted rules of academic writing are still in place even when the assignment is called "creative." This makes creative writing in academic settings far more predictable than commercial creative writing.

In fact, you could argue that academic creative writing is not all that creative, having pre-determined structures and components. Yet it flourishes: narrative essays, assigned short stories and plays, and poetry written for a course are all forms of academic creative writing.

If you have an assignment to write creatively for an academic class, you should be aware of the typical analytical elements that will be used to evaluate what you write (your text):

- *Plot* (events, in some order);

- *Characters* (human and non-human);

- *Setting* (time and place);

- *Point-of-view* (who is telling the story?);

- *Imagery and symbolism* (imagery includes tropes such as metaphors and similes that convey meaning in nonliteral ways; symbols are words or tropes that stand for or indicate certain ideas and events);

- *Mood* (how the reader feels about the text) and tone (how the writer feels about the text);

- *Theme* (what point is the writer trying to make? Theme is often expressed in tropes and symbols).

Even if you, the writer, have not taken these conventions into account, professors will use them when they evaluate and grade your creative writing efforts. These conventions are strong in academia, so it's wise to look at what you write and identify these elements to be sure they are recognizably in place.

Poetry: Condensed Meaning

Poetry may seem like a strange foreign language that is impossible to understand. Most poetry is written almost in code: arresting images are used to open the reader's mind, meaningful symbols take the place of straightforward language, and conventional sentence structure is so changed as to be unrecognizable.

But truly, poems can be analyzed like other literary texts. Most of the poems you will encounter in academia are built on the elements listed above. The trick is to observe how these elements are used to create striking and memorable images and to arouse your emotions while using a minimum of words. Good poetry strips away clichéd images and excessive words, leaving just the barest bones of significance and meaning.

If you are asked to write poetry, try to let your imagination run free. What kind of pictures does your mind offer up? Put these images into words—as few words as possible. There, you've written a poem.

Analyzing a poem that someone else has written is not harder than analyzing a short story. Look for the standard elements listed above, making notes on any really obscure lines. Use a dictionary if needed, remembering that most poems use words "poetically"—that is, not confining their meaning to strict definitions.

Poetry aims first at the ear, then the heart, then the mind. If a poem simply won't reveal itself to you, read it out loud. What do you feel when you hear the words? Don't be concerned if your feelings seem not to match the exact words—the beauty of poetry, like music, is that it plucks strings in your soul in non-rational ways. Even in academia, there is a place for feelings and emotions!

How to become a better writer, the hard way!

Writing is used in all kinds of settings for a tremendous variety of purposes. Academic writing adheres to certain standards, expectations, rules, and conventions that might be completely inappropriate in business, for example. The good news is that the standards you are learning in this book are widely published and accepted in academia, so you don't have to guess how to do it right.

The chief skills you need to write well in academic settings are to recognize what you are being asked to write and to have enough models of various kinds of academic writing to match the assignment to the steps needed to produce the right text.

As with any skill, you need to learn the basics, to practice and get feedback on your performance, and to improve as you learn better, more effective, more accurate, and more appropriate ways of performing. In this regard, writing is like baking, planting a garden, skiing, surfing, dancing, playing the piano, playing pool, singing, wood-carving, knitting, or any other skill-based activity.

Natural talent is a boost, of course, but I have seen students with very modest natural writing talent become excellent writers. They decided that they would improve, they put in the hard work, and they were rewarded with better grades and the satisfaction of accomplishment. These students set aside time to read and write like a professor, and their skills grew as they used them. You can achieve the same!

Activities for academic and creative writing

1. Write an academic essay

   - Choose any reading from *The Professor's Book of Readings*.

   - Using all your close reading techniques, read and annotate the reading.

   - Use the prewriting strategies to prepare for writing.

   - Write about the reading using one of the prompts that goes with the reading.

   - Get feedback; revise and rewrite till the essay is polished and as perfect as you can make it.

2. Creative writing: The Memoir

   - Choose a memoir from *The Professor's Book of Readings*.

   - Using it as a model, write your own memoir, focused on one event in your life.

- Get feedback; revise and rewrite till the memoir is as polished and perfect as you can make it.

3. Creative writing: Poetry

- Choose a poem from *The Professor's Book of Readings*.

- Read the poem out loud. Poetry is meant to be heard, not read on a page.

- What do you hear in the poem? Is there rhythm? Rhyme?

- Does the poem conjure any images (pictures) in your mind?

- Write a poetry mimic. Copy the length, rhythms, and rhyme scheme of the poem, substituting your own topic, images, and symbols.

- Share your mimic and see what kind of feedback you get.

Chapter Three: Getting it all together: having confidence in yourself as an effective communicator

Chapter Highlights

- Take yourself seriously as a reader, writer, speaker, and listener

- Writing well is the best way to develop all your communication skills

- Pay attention to feedback: editing and revising your writing

- Commitment to continuous improvement

Take yourself seriously as a reader, writer, speaker, and listener

We humans are, from birth, communicators. Infants communicate through all-over body language, tears, giggles, and facial expressions. The people around them communicate back in the same ways, reinforcing the baby's communication skills by responding to and imitating what the baby does. This shows the baby that communication is a two-way street.

Speaking and listening (along with observing) are the main means of communicating in the early years of human life. These skills are being perfected constantly, as infants and the people around them receive feedback and modify their performance based on what works well (gets the desired result) and what seems ineffective. For most people, speaking and listening dominate the first years of life.

Then, in early childhood, humans begin the arduous tasks of learning to read and write. It's debatable whether the best order for learning these skills is to teach reading first. Montessori schools, for example, often begin with writing. The reasoning is that children learn the alphabet by writing, making it easier to learn to read as they already recognize the letters in words.

But no matter how reading and writing are taught, they are closely related skills. Both involve recognizing words and understanding how they are combined to express ideas. Both use sophisticated skills that develop rapidly as they are practiced. Both are crucial to exchanging information and ideas with other people.

Sentences contain words arranged in certain patterns to convey meaning; in this way, the words expand beyond their own particular denotation (literal meaning) and are used to communicate abstract concepts. For example, take the sentence "Life is good." Each word has a particular meaning, but the sentence as a whole goes beyond just the words to generate an attitude about life.

This is where the power of reading and writing becomes clear. By arranging words in ways that paint images or point to conclusions, writing communicates complex perceptions. By reading such writing, the reader is stimulated to think about both the literal and the abstract meaning of the words. In this exchange, both readers and writers generate ideas and compare information; they have a "silent conversation" on a topic of interest. Even if readers and writers are centuries apart in time or thousands of miles apart in distance, they can talk to each other!

Of course, humans never stop using their first skills— speaking and listening. Theoretically, you could move through life just speaking and listening, without perfecting reading and writing skills. However, it's quite likely you will never develop your communication skills to the highest level if you do not read and write well.

What reading and writing do is refashion the brain. As we struggle to understand what we read and to write with clarity and precision, we build our ability to think logically and systematically, to organize our thoughts and ideas, and to see how new information ties in with what's already known. We learn how to discern the weak spots of an argument (our own or someone else's) and how to use other people's writing to support our own ideas. We become aware of the human tendency not to challenge our own thinking by noticing how writers may overlook obvious holes in their own logic. We see how some writers use sweeping generalizations (prejudices and stereotypes) in their writing. When we are not convinced by the writer's arguments, we start to see similar weak places in our own thinking and writing.

In addition, reading and writing are the most natural ways to build your vocabulary. If you try to memorize lists of words with definitions, you'll probably find that you forget them right away. In contrast, encountering new words as you read gives you clues and context that help you figure out what the words mean and how to use them correctly and effectively.

As a writer, you often ponder to clarify what you really want to say. Part of the clarification process may be using the thesaurus to find just the right word. It's likely you'll remember that word after going to so much trouble to find it!

Reading and writing help you organize your thinking, learn new words, and become critical of your own weaknesses in using logic to support an idea. These skills will boost your ability to speak effectively—to get the results you seek when you speak. In listening, too, your expanded skill set makes you better able to hear when a speaker has lost the thread of their argument and is simply repeating words to keep the audience listening. You can follow the organization of a spoken lecture much more easily when you know the basics of good writing.

In sum, reading and writing provide and develop vital abilities and strategies that will elevate your speaking and listening skills. Reading and writing well can sharpen your ability to concentrate as you listen and to drive home a point with style and strength when you speak.

Writing well is the best way to develop all your communication skills

For many people, writing never stops being difficult and exhausting. There are so many words, and how can you choose just the right ones, put them in the right order, and produce writing that expresses what you really want to say?

In truth, all writing is hard. Even experienced writers have dry spells where they cannot think of anything to write about. They force themselves to write, but what they write is dull, flat, stale, and not at all compelling,

It's easy to feel that your writer's voice is stifled by the problems, situations, and circumstances around you. But from my personal experience, I've found that writing is the best way to sort through my emotions, ideas, half-formed thoughts, and fears about my life.

Somehow, the process of turning the swirling mass in my brain into cool, crisp words makes things more manageable. The effort of finding words that correctly express my inner life helps me sort out the vague and unsettling notions that are distracting me from understanding and appreciating what's really happening around me.

In a way, writing is a cheap form of therapy that you do with yourself. Writing that you never publish (make public) can be transformative. It's private, and you can clearly express what you could not quite think through or say to someone else.

Writing begins to fulfill its potential only when someone else reads it. When your professor, friend, family member, teacher, counselor, or romantic partner (or wider audience of social media friends and strangers) reads your writing, you have gone public. Other people can read what you wrote and react accordingly. You hope that what you say makes sense and is helpful, but once it's out there, it's out there.

And here is where writing really shines. If you can gather from your readers their reaction—their feedback, their counter-arguments, their opinion—then you have completed the task of all written communication: the writer writes, the reader reads, and both engage in a conversation.

This takes us back to Chapter One, where we thought about the connection between reading and writing. First you read, then you write. Then someone reads what you wrote, using those close reading techniques. They respond, you write back—the communication grows and changes everyone's thinking.

Writers do not have all the answers. They often start with only a very tiny idea or insight. But that's all it takes to build a piece of writing that will reverberate for years to come.

Pay attention to feedback: editing and revising your writing

The writer's best friend is an honest, competent editor. As you develop your skills as a writer by reading other writer's works and incorporating the feedback you get from professors, teachers, friends, and friendly critics, you build your arsenal of skills. You become familiar with your own writerly voice and can hear when you sound inauthentic or careless. You become your own first editor; if you are lucky, you'll find more editors.

In most college courses, your professor becomes your editor. The grade you receive is feedback on how well you performed in the assignment:

- Following directions;

- Using standard grammar, punctuation, spelling and capitalization;

- Organizing the writing so that the reader can follow your logic;

- Having something to say: hopefully, your ideas are original and compelling!

If you are in college, and your professor has 150 students or more, you may find that the grade is not explained. There are no corrections, suggestions, or reactions written on the paper—just the grade.

You could approach your professor and ask nicely if you can get some feedback. This might begin a valuable relationship that will help you improve your writing in significant ways.

Another strategy is to find a writing consultant or tutor. Some colleges and universities provide them to students for free. If you can't find help for free, you could hire your own tutor. If you're lucky, you may work with your tutor for years, getting personal attention and recommendations based on your writing style and the needs of your classes.

If you decide to publish what you write, you may hire an editor. Developmental editors work on the broad issues faced at the beginning of a writing task: what do you want to achieve with your writing? Who is your audience, and how can you reach them?

Copy editors look at finished work, concentrating on the development, organization, and impact of the work. Line editors look at the minutia: spelling, punctuation, sentence structure problems, and lapses in coherence of the piece of writing.

Should you self-publish or sell your work to a commercial publisher? Here you need to consider ownership, editing, marketing, and royalty payments to you, the author.

1. When you make a contract with a commercial publisher, you are selling your work. You no longer own it. You can't change it, publish it yourself, or control how the publisher uses it. The publisher may change the title, ask you to rewrite sections, or decide not to publish it at all. Since the publisher owns the work, you have nothing to say about these decisions unless you managed to get them into the contract; usually, first-time authors haven't got the clout to do so.

2. You may have a line or copy editor assigned to your work, but often that person is quite stretched with other authors and can't pay as much attention as you might like. In the long run, this is not a free editor; you will pay for this editing through the significant

percentage the publisher takes from your earnings as a writer.

3. You may expect that your publisher will market your published book, envisioning tours, signings, and all kinds of publicity. In reality, such red-carpet treatment is reserved for authors who are reliable-money makers, not first-time authors. Marketing may become your responsibility.

4. Many contracts include an advance to the author. This is not free money! The publisher expects that your work will earn back the advance. If this does not happen (your work does not produce sufficient sales, movie rights, etc.), then you owe the publisher money. You may be asked to write more books to try to pay back that money.

5. Royalties are the money the publisher pays to the author after the advance is "earned out." Typically, first-time authors earn a royalty of 5-7% of what the work earns.

6. Self-publishing on platforms like Amazon avoids all these circumstances, but brings its own problems: editing, marketing, distribution, and accounting are all the responsibility of the author.

Of course, you can always self-publish in a blog, a Facebook post, or a tweet. Who reads your writing and how much money you earn this way depends on your business skills in marketing and finding sponsors—companies that will pay you for the privilege of advertising on your social media sites.

Commitment to continuous improvement

Any set of skills will lapse if you don't use them. Playing the piano, making goals in soccer, speaking a foreign language, baking bread, riding a horse, writing in cursive script—all of these skills need to be practiced to stay sharp.

But practice alone is not enough. You can reach a level of competency in any skill, then stay there. You are stuck. How to move beyond being stuck?

- Find people more skilled than you, then ask for or pay for lessons;

- Read books, attend workshops and training camps, and take more classes;

- Teach a class—there's no better way to find out what you actually know than to teach someone else;

- If you speak one or several languages other than English, you can raise your English skills to a much higher level by taking on translating or interpreting work. Translators and interpreters use all four communication skill-sets: listening, speaking, reading, and writing. As you translate words from one language to another, you learn valuable lessons about using words carefully and correctly. Even words that seem to mean the same thing are not exactly equivalent.

Taking into account connotation, context, and nuance are critical to competent translation. In this way, you build your mastery of English communication skills.

- Move into new ways of seeing the skills; be original in how you practice and develop your communication skills.

Professors of reading and writing often publish their own writings. This is an act of courage, as no one is above being criticized, often harshly. Academics are notorious for their severe treatment of each other's work.

To survive in the competitive arena of academic writing, you need a thick skin, a sense of proportion, and an on-going determination to improve your communication skills. The ability to articulate your position with diplomacy and tact is a laudable goal for any professor. In academic writing, it's especially important to be fair, firm, frank, and friendly. Learning this skill-set is a challenge for professors, so don't be surprised when it takes you much time, practice, and ability to accept criticism (not all of which is meant constructively!) in order to experience significant improvement in your own communication skills.

No one is perfect when it comes to reading or writing. Each of us brings our own past failures and triumphs, our preconceptions and prejudices, our stereotypes and hasty conclusions with us when we read and write. We all suffer from bias (unfounded judgments about certain things), and not one of us can read and write with perfect objectivity.

Yet professors are certain that it's worth the struggle to become better at what we do. We read, we write, we gather feedback, we revise, and we repeat the process. We are not finished products—and that's a good thing! As the world changes around us, we are called on to find new ways of communicating. A commitment to continuous improvement is what is takes to read and write like a professor.

Here are a few guidelines for setting up your own continuous improvement plan.

1. *Be self-directed.* Realize that you (not your teacher, your family, or your friends) are in charge of your learning. When you don't do as well as you had intended on a particular assignment, take the time to analyze where you went wrong. Pay particular attention to that weak spot. How can you strengthen your performance in the future?

2. *Use resources effectively.* If you are taking a class, the teacher and the texts are primary resources. Libraries and the Internet (used wisely) are key resources. The people around you are also resources, just as you are a resource for them. Study groups with fellow students can be solid gold opportunities to give and receive help and encouragement.

3. *Manage your time well.* Find your most productive time and use that time for energy-draining activities like

reading and writing. Allow yourself enough time on an assignment not to feel rushed.

4.   *Be self-reflective.* How do you learn best? Alone, in a quiet place, or with some hubbub around you? Do you want to see information or hear it? How important is it to build in active moments as you work?

To read and write like a professor takes a lifetime. Most professors have gone to school for 29 years or more, and they don't stop learning at any point along the way!

You can decide today that you will be a life-long learner. Don't tell yourself that your communication skills are "good enough" as they are.

Include reading and writing in your daily activities. Just like physical exercise, spending an hour a day in reading and writing activities can keep your skills sharp, help you improve as you evaluate your performance, and keep you motivated to reach for continuous improvement.

Activities for getting it all together

1. Write a short autobiography about your life as a communicator. Imagine yourself as a baby—did you make a lot of noise? Were you good at mimicking people? Did you feel that you got plenty of attention? Then think about learning to read and write. Was it easy for you, or did you struggle to keep up with your teacher and classmates? How did these early experiences influence your self-image and your abilities as a communicator?

2. Think about yourself right now. Are you an effective communicator? Do you know how to get your point across in speaking and writing? When you read, do you give the writer your full attention? Are you a good listener, according to other people? Can you keep your mind focused on what someone is saying, or are you easily distracted? How can you improve your communication skills?

3. Is there anything in your life that consumes your attention? That is, is there something you wish you knew everything about? Do you read according to whim or with purpose? Think about how you approach learning. Are you systematic, or do you collect as much information as possible, sorting it out later? Consider how you can become more expert in those areas of interest and how you can communicate, as a writer, what you have learned.

Appendix A: Basic tools for reading and writing. Developing a thesis. Annotation, outline, summary, analysis

Thesis

Your thesis is the spine of your composition. The thesis is your main point: what you are arguing or claiming to be true. Your reader should be able to easily identify your thesis, as it is the main guidepost in your paper.

Nearly every academic paper is argumentative and requires an argumentative thesis. The thesis must be "arguable" in that you have made a statement, or claim, about your topic that is not simply factual. The statement must be one with which reasonable people could disagree.

If all you have are facts, then you have an informational thesis, not an argumentative thesis.

Here's an example of an argumentative thesis:

- TOPIC: Global warming will change the ecosystems of the planet.

- YOUR CLAIM: The pace of global warming is accelerating

- THESIS: As the pace of global warming accelerates, there will be corresponding changes in the ecosystems of the planet.

How is this thesis debatable? Some people will agree that the pace is accelerating; other will not. And some people will dispute the existence of global warming.

How can you support this thesis? Data, scientific studies, recent facts and charts, and personal experience can all be used to validate this thesis.

Focus, unity, and good supporting details are key elements in a well-written argumentative essay. The thesis is what holds it all together. As you develop your argumentative thesis, you will need to find credible support.

Your thesis will keep you focused on one claim and prevent your paper from straying into new ideas that will distract and confuse the reader.

Annotation, outline, summary, and analysis

These four skill areas have much in common. All of them require the reader to do a *close reading* of a text and locate the key information.

Close Reading consists of reading in depth and searching for the most important information in a text. It often requires more than one reading of a text to digest all the information provided and pick out the key themes and ideas.

Mastering the four skill areas will help you in your entire college career, so take the time to learn how to engage with a text and draw out essential information.

Annotation

Annotation is taking notes on the text. It is a process of identifying only and all of the most important points of the text. You can either write directly on the text or takes notes on a separate piece of paper. When you annotate, take special notice of these parts of the text:

- *First sentence of each paragraph* (this is usually the topic sentence);

- *Anything in bold:* words or phrases that may be definitions or key terms;

- *The first and last paragraphs.* Here you can usually find the thesis (main point).

Don't use a highlighter for annotating, as it will tempt you to mark complete sentences rather than individual points. A page covered with yellow highlighter is not useful! It does not distinguish what is important and why.

Instead, make up a code: you can circle dates, underline names, and put key points into little boxes. Write a question mark in the margin to note something you don't understand or want to follow up. Experiment to find an annotation method that works for you.

Outline

Outlines help you construct the essentials of organization: creating an introduction and thesis, developing paragraphs, and writing a powerful conclusion.

For researched papers, study your annotated resources and decide which pieces of information best support the specific points of your thesis. Then arrange the pieces of information (direct quotes and paraphrases) in outline form.

Here is a basic outline format:

I. Introduction

•   In the first sentence, make a general introductory statement. This will introduce the topic and engage the reader's attention:

_____

•   Provide some context and background for the reader:

_____

•   Begin to move toward your thesis:

_____

•   Thesis statement:

_____

II. Body Paragraph 1

- Topic Sentence. *Everything in the paragraph must relate to this sentence*:

  _____

- Supporting Sentences (details from research or your own experience):

  _____

  _____

  _____

- Concluding or Transitional Sentence. Wraps up the paragraph and/or points to the next paragraph:

  _____

III. Body Paragraph 2

- Topic Sentence. *Everything in the paragraph must relate to this sentence*:

  _____

- Supporting Sentences (details from research or your own experience):

  _____

  _____

  _____

- Concluding or Transitional Sentence. Wraps up the paragraph and/or points to the next paragraph:

  _____

IV. Body Paragraph 3

- Topic Sentence. *Everything in the paragraph must relate to this sentence:*

  _____

- Supporting Sentences (details from research or your own experience):

  _____

  _____

  _____

- Concluding or Transitional Sentence. Wraps up the paragraph and/or points to the next paragraph:

  _____

V. Conclusion

- Restate the thesis BUT in different words and syntax:

  _____

- Summarize the main points you discussed in your

  body paragraphs; consider rewriting topic sentences of

  your body paragraphs in different words and syntax:

  _____

  _____

  _____

- Concluding Sentence. Let the reader know you have

  proven your thesis—the final touch!

  _____

Summary

Summarizing is writing the most important points of the text as a paragraph or series of paragraphs. The summary will be shorter than the original text, maybe 1/3 as long. It will not include examples or illustrations but may include a definition if it's crucial to the reader's understanding of the text.

The tone of the summary is impersonal; do not allow your opinion to creep into a summary. Try to stick to the bare bones of the text, giving your reader just the most essential information.

A *paraphrase* is a specific type of summary. It is used when you are using a resource to support your own writing, as in a research paper or researched essay. A paraphrase summarizes an important point made by the author of the resource using your own words. You could use a direct quotation for this purpose; a paraphrase is most often used when you want to summarize several points at the same time or have instructions from your professor to limit the number of direct quotations. Paraphrasing requires that you understand both the meaning of the material you are using and how it supports your own argument.

Analysis

In an analysis, you move beyond summarizing the main points of a text into making statements as to the writer's purpose and the meaning of the text.

Analysis is a common procedure in many academic areas. Chemists analyze chemical compounds. Musicians analyze musical scores. Mathematicians analyze algebraic equations. Statisticians analyze trends in data they have gathered. And students analyze written texts!

You use skills of analysis in daily life when you compare prices while shopping, decide on what college to attend, think about what your friend just said to you, or try to figure out the best way to get from here to there.

Good analysis proceeds in steps:

1. *Gather data* (facts, past experiences, words, ideas, and your own intuition)

2. *Organize the data* (turn a mish-mosh into orderly groupings)

3. *Look for patterns* in the data (when A happens, does B always follow? What conditions seem to influence outcomes?)

4. *Make conclusions* based on the patterns (what does it all mean? How can I express what I am seeing?)

We make many analytical judgments without thinking consciously.

For example, you meet someone new. Usually, you decide right away if you like or don't like them. How do you decide? You use many analytical tools such as how the person dresses or speaks, if the person reminds you of someone else, the setting where you meet, and so on. But most of these tools are used without you realizing you are using them. In this case, your analysis may be too hasty or flawed, leading to a poor decision.

In academic analysis, you must move slowly and deliberately when you perform an analysis. For example, a professor may ask you to analyze a character in a story. If you are in a hurry, you may read one or two things the character says or does and make some statements about why they did what they did.

Then you get your grade from your professor—and the grade is not good! The professor tells you that you have not been thorough in using all the four steps noted above. Maybe you didn't gather enough data, or you organized it poorly. Next time, be sure to devote sufficient attention to gathering and organizing data before you attempt an analysis.

Consider how to improve your skills of analysis. In any academic setting, constant and efficient analysis is expected. You will not get far as a student without the ability to write effective, correct analyses when you review data.

The Big Four

These four skill areas discussed above are the foundation of all academic writing. No matter what graduate school or career path you are considering, you will not get far unless you can do these things with efficiency and consistency:

1. Annotate a text;

2. Outline a paper before you start writing it;

3. Summarize key information;

4. Analyze what you are writing about, creating new insights for the reader.

Appendix B: The Essay and its genres

What is an essay?

The French word "essay" means "to try." An essay is an initial attempt to convey what the writer thinks about a topic. These first thoughts are expressed in somewhat tentative ideas, not sturdy fortresses of words. There is a freedom in writing essays that is not found in most academic writing, which is heavily fact-based and not very concerned with style or with the reader's conclusions.

More weighty types of academic writing such as dissertations, graduate theses, research papers, literature reviews, and reports have value based on the degree to which they prove their points. They persuade the reader mainly by providing so much proof that the reader can only dispute their conclusions by writing another research-based piece that uses other experts, data, statistics, and experimental results to prove the reader's opposing points. Academic papers at the graduate and professional levels have much in common with legal arguments or battle plans: they depend on relevant, verifiable facts to make them strong.

Essays, on the other hand, rely on the writer's skill to make their point. There are dozens of genres (types) of essays, but all depend on the writer's ability to engage, persuade, or capture the attention of the reader long enough to make a point.

While most academic writing is logical, rather dry, factual, and emotionless, essays can be charming, diverting, and light-hearted. They can be intensely personal and opinionated without the need to support the writer's opinions.

However, there is one notable exception to the idea of an essay as a somewhat loose form of academic writing. In many colleges and universities, your professor may say "essay" when what they mean is "researched essay."

The researched essay is a hybrid, combining the less-rigorous, more exploratory approach of the essay with the heavier demands of the traditional research paper. It requires a formal thesis, usually argumentative, combined with correctly-documented expert opinion (taken from credible, reliable resources) to prove a relatively narrow point.

Be sure to clarify what genre your professor has in mind when they assign an essay. Look for key words in the assignment, especially verbs: define, investigate, recall, and so on.

Essay genres

Here are some of the most commonly-assigned genres of academic essays. Please bear in mind that these genres may overlap, and that professors may assign a genre by a different name than this list provides.

1. *Argumentative*: has a thesis (arguable point, not just a topic) and body paragraphs that logically support the thesis. The introductory and concluding paragraphs offer general remarks and context concerning the thesis. You may be called on to provide a counterargument paragraph in which you state the strengths of an opposing view of the topic. Some argumentative essays may require research, as noted above in the "researched essay."

2. *Persuasive*: seeks to persuade the reader that a particular position is correct or preferable. It is much like the argumentative essay, though it may not rely so much on logical support—emotional appeals may be used.

3. *Descriptive*: here, the writer focuses on describing a person, place, or event. Often, imagery and symbolic language are used. The essay may be personal, describing the writer's experiences, or literary, describing a character or place in a short story or novel.

4. *Narrative*: this essay tells a story. It traces an event or idea from some starting point through changes or developments. The end usually has a lesson or moral. Memoirs are a kind of narrative essay; they often focus on one specific event, a kind of epiphany or "ah-ha!" moment in a person's life.

5. *Definition*: here, the writer defines a specific thing, event, idea, or concept. Often, outside sources are used to provide facts and data. Be careful not to lapse into a laundry list of definitions or a simple review of facts unless the assignment calls for such an approach.

6. *Compare-contrast*: a common essay genre, this is based on identifying similar or dissimilar elements in two or

more different things. The elements are compared (how are they alike?) and/or contrasted (how are they different?). These essays can be quite detailed and elaborate. There are several customary ways to organize this essay genre, so look closely at your professor's instructions.

7. *Exemplification*: these essays make a concept or idea clear by illustrating it with examples that the reader can envision and understand. This is not a common genre in academia.

8. *Expository*: in this genre, a specific idea is explored and made clear to the reader by use of examples, data, or other kinds of illustration.

Different professors may use different words for these genres, depending on where and when they went to graduate school. Like so many things in life, essay genres go in and out of fashion.

Sometimes professors become so familiar with their own assignments that they forget to clearly indicate the genre of the essay. If you are confused or unsure about what kind of essay to write, read all the instructions several times. Talk with a classmate or tutor to get their opinions.

But remember, your professor will be grading your essay, so if you want to be very sure you are writing using the correct genre, ask your professor for clarification. Ask specific question that show you have read the instructions so that your professor can best reply and clarify what they expect from you.

Essays are thinking exercises. They give writers the chance to express thoughts and ideas which may not be proven or widely accepted. Good essays spark discussion and open paths of exploration. Becoming a skilled essayist is a worthy goal for any writer.

Acknowledgements

First, I want to thank my students from all around the world. Over the past four decades, they have taught me how to teach writing and reading. Whenever I come up with a great new way to present the materials they need to know, they come up with great new ways to do it their own way (not necessarily the way I had in mind!).

This back-and-forth communication shows me, in a clear and practical way, what works and what does not in my teaching. I take out my revising tools and make incremental changes till I have a method and strategy for teaching a particular facet of reading and writing that speaks to all my students.

I also want to thank my exceptional teachers, not all of whom taught English. My elementary teachers taught me the fundamentals of grammar: thanks to Mrs. Coley and Mrs. Carlyle. Junior and Senior high school teachers who stand out in my memory are Mrs. Merrill, Ms. Porter, Ms. Harrod and Mr. West. At Potsdam College, my Sociology and History professors guided me into sticking to the point and not adding fluff; Dr. Turbett, Dr. Nadel, Dr. Johnson, and Dr. McLaughlin were especially helpful in curbing my wordiness.

In my career, colleagues who have been influential include Professor Jean-Paul Swiatkowski, Dr. Paul Hacker, and my writing buddy, grad student and fellow tutor Liz Trepanier.

My first-line editors are my husband Jarda and my children, Noah and Melissa. I expect that soon my granddaughter will join the ranks of those who read and correct me!

And I also want to thank the thousands of authors whose books I have read. They wormed their way into my head, my heart, and my soul, showing me the myriad ways

of putting together words. Their friendship through the

written page has been fundamental in my own

development as a reader and writer.

About the Author

Born in Kentucky, Sara Tusek has lived in Prague, Boston, New York, Colorado, Tennessee, and Florida. She is a writer and educator. Over the past four decades, Sara has worked with thousands of people from all over the world, helping them improve key academic skills and inspiring them to fulfill their own potential as students and in their careers.

Sara writes novels, including *Prague for Beginners*, and short stories, as well as books, how-to manuals, and articles on individual career development, trends in international business, and improving English-language communication skills. She holds a Master's Degree in Education from Vanderbilt University and has extensive experience in sociological and historical research, curriculum development, and cross-cultural relations. Sara served as career counselor at St Lawrence University and directed the career services office at The University of the South.

Sara and her husband Jaroslav run the International Leadership Institute (ILI), which has been helping executives and students develop their leadership, English, and career skills since 1985. The Institute worked with the Czech government to develop leadership development programs from 1991-1995; from 1996-2006, the Institute worked with the US Department of State in its AID programs. Sara founded and directs the American English Language Institute, a division of ILI.

From 2010-2013, ILI's main offices were in Prague, where Sara ran American English Language Institute programs for South Korean, Ukrainian, Vietnamese, Czech, and Slovak participants. Instruction focused on academic writing and reading skill development, as well as preparing for university admission.

In the US, Sara has worked with international college students from the Caribbean; Africa; Central, South, and North America; Central and Eastern Europe; and East Asia to develop their ease and confidence in reading, writing, speaking, and listening to American English.

The Tuseks divide their time between Prague and Florida. They have two children, Noah and Melissa, a daughter-in-law, Tina, and a grandchild, Amelia.

You can visit the International Leadership website at www.ili.cc.

NOTES

NOTES

NOTES

NOTES

NOTES

NOTES

NOTES

NOTES

NOTES

NOTES

NOTES

NOTES

NOTES

NOTES

NOTES

NOTES

NOTES

NOTES

NOTES

NOTES

NOTES

NOTES

NOTES

NOTES

NOTES

NOTES

NOTES

NOTES

NOTES

NOTES

NOTES

NOTES

NOTES

NOTES

NOTES

www.ingramcontent.com/pod-product-compliance
Lightning Source LLC
Chambersburg PA
CBHW070635030426
42337CB00020B/4016